I0786864

CELESTIAL RUNE SIGILS

Elder Futhark BindRunes

All Natural Spirit

Copyright © 2020 All Natural Spirit

All rights reserved

No part of this book may be reproduced, or stored in a retrieval system,
or transmitted in any form or by any means, electronic, mechanical,
photocopying, recording, or otherwise, without express written permission
of the publisher.

ISBN-13: 9798664967579

Cover design by: All Natural Spirit

CONTENTS

LIST OF BOOKS IN THIS SERIES

Runes Book 1: *Runic Evolution and Linguistic History, The Origin of the Germanic Runes & Universal Rune Sets* by All Natural Spirit (2020).

Runes Book 3: *Elder Futhark Arcanum: An Intuitive Interpretation of Rune Meanings* by All Natural Spirit (2021).

For more information, please see the Books in this Series section at the end of the book.

PREFACE

I have been researching the runic alphabets extensively for the last few years and they have become a prominent feature on my website (https://allnaturalspirit.com). They have been a source of inspiration for several scholarly articles and have been distilled into oracle decks, print-on-demand art and now several books! My fascination with this ancient writing script seems far from spent as I constantly develop innovative techniques and products to utilize the runes to gain wisdoms from the collective consciousness as well as the depth of our own souls.

CELESTIAL RUNE SIGILS DECK

My studies into the Elder Futhark, which have fascinated me since childhood, have been converted into a coherent system of BindRunes for everyday use without the requirement of expert knowledge.

My BindRune project, named the Celestial Rune Sigils (The Metaphysician's Toolbox) has transformed into a deck of 24 black and white cards, representative of their origins from the 24 Elder Futhark Runes, with details on their crafting, uses and invocation.

The Old English Rune Poem is used as a descriptive guide for the Elder Futhark using 24 stanzas. Similarly, the Celestial Rune Sigils contain keywords and short verses on each card to describe the intention for each BindRune. It has taken me years to create this set of 24 BindRunes, as I wanted the deck to develop at its own pace, which would ensure quality and authenticity. It is not a divinatory deck, but rather it has a more active role with each card having a specific intention and contribution towards metaphysical, spiritual and magickal rituals.

Therefore, the deck is not restricted to tarot readers or oracle enthusiasts. It has been created for the larger metaphysical community and would be of special interest to our energy workers and magick wielders. It would be appropriate for most ages, including the very young and those who are wiser (primarily 18-40+ years), since it can be used as a personal deck and as a deck to assist clients during various healing or magick sessions. This deck also makes a great travel companion.

For more information about the deck, please visit my website.

❋ ❋ ❋

INTRODUCTION

This book was inspired by the Celestial Rune Sigils (The Metaphysician's Toolbox) deck. Similarly it contains 24 black and white Elder Futhark BindRunes or sigils of my own creation. Interpretation and use of the sigils does not require previous or expert knowledge of the Elder Futhark runes, since each sigil has been designed to be self-explanatory, however this book contains additional guidance for the usage of each or their visualization during invocation.

We start our journey with the definition of Runes and BindRunes to provide some background information. After which I discuss the additional elements that I use in the sigil construction process. We discuss each of the 24 sigils in turn, which includes its name, poem, the order in which to draw the runes that make up the sigils along with any additional alchemical symbols, the meaning behind the BindRune and finally its potential metaphysical use. I conclude the booklet with overview tables for each of the BindRunes.

❉ ❉ ❉

WHAT ARE THE RUNES?

Strictly speaking; the runes collectively represent the earliest of alphabets and primitive writing systems, such that letters can be easily carved into wood or stone using a blade or mallet and chisel.

Three of the most ancient writing scripts are the Runic Alphabets. The Elder Futhark, Anglo Saxon Futhorc and Younger Futhark are descendants from the Germanic tribes and the Proto-Germanic language. The origins of these runes as well as their universal rune representations are discussed in my first book of this series; *Runic Evolution and Linguistic History, The Origin of the Germanic Runes & Universal Rune Sets* by All Natural Spirit (2020).

The most interesting aspect of the runes is their modern use in divination and magickal rituals. Here rituals refer to a set of steps through which you facilitate self-development, such as the burning of candles or incense during meditation – setting the spiritual mood as it were. BindRunes play a very important role in the magickal aspect of runes and are a doorway to practicing creative expression and facilitating creative problem solving.

✽ ✽ ✽

WHAT ARE BINDRUNES?

BindRunes are rune combination, which is speculated to have been initially used for the initials of the carver's name (Figure 1). BindRunes are generally 2 – 3 runes joined together to form a glyph (i.e., writing used to indicate a specific meaning) using a common vertical anchor point. They are common for the Anglo-Saxon Futhorc, but there are representatives for the Elder Futhark and Younger Futhark as well.

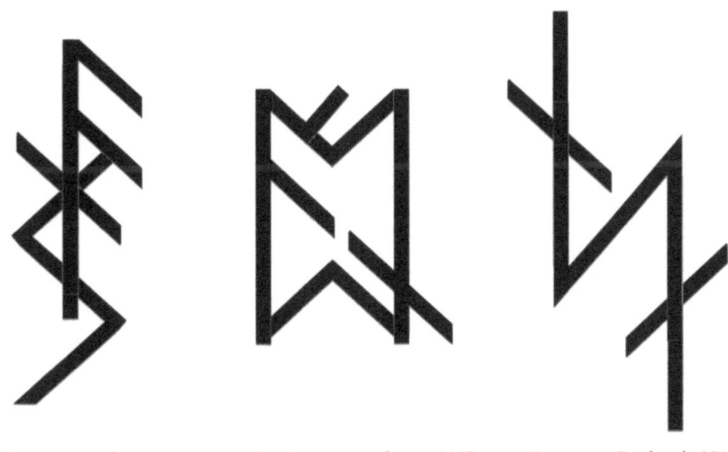

Elder Futhark ANS   Anglo-Saxon Futhorc ANS   Younger Futhark ANS

Figure 1: Examples of three different BindRunes from the Elder Futhark, Anglo-Saxon Futhorc and Younger Futhark depicting ANS for All Natural Spirit. They utilise a common vertical line and thus they represent rune glyphs.

The creation of BindRunes is not limited to ancient inscriptions, many hobbyists and metaphysicians have also created their own set of BindRunes, specifically to combine the metaphysical properties of the runes. The Celestial Rune Sigils contain a set of BindRunes of my own design.

* * *

WHAT ARE THE CELESTIAL RUNE SIGILS?

Each of the Celestial Rune Sigil contains a BindRune of 3-4 runes from the Elder Futhark. They are not glyphs in the traditional sense as they do not always anchor the runes on a common vertical line. Therefore, I have opted to call them sigils; which are magickal symbols that represent the practitioner's desired outcome.

The Elder Futhark is a set of 24 Germanic alphabet discovered in Gotland (1903) on the Kylver Stone that dates back to 400 AD. Minimalist Elder Futhark BindRunes were the foundation of the deck and this book to ensure clear intention for each Sigil. For example the Enlightenment Sigil represents personal empowerment and magic, the Weapon of Light Sigil converts shades during shadow work and the Space Sigil creates an environment conducive to meditation. Therefore, the Sigils were designed to incorporate the least number of runes as to not muddle the message. Simplicity is the key to creating tools that work well for a specific purpose.

Some Sigils contain additional alchemical symbols of Fire, Air, Water and Earth to strengthen the original meaning. The Weapon - and Shield of Light Sigils gain extra power through their connection to the cosmic/universal current (Figure 2). More detail about the cosmic or universal current is provided in the Journey of the Weapon of Light Sigil section.

Figure 2: The alchemical symbol for the cosmic or universal current.

* * *

THE CELESTIAL RUNE SIGILS: AN ELDER FUTHARK BINDRUNE SET

Journey of the Celestial Rune Sigils

The Elder Futhark runes can be used as both a divinatory (passive) and magickal (active) tool. I personally use them for the latter, where I actively participate in setting the intention that I seek.

I use the runes extensively for my shadow work, creative problem solving and spiritual rituals. Hence they have become a spiritual tool with which I explore the depths of soul and to introduce some light and magick into my everyday hum-drum life.

As stated before, no previous or expert knowledge is required to use my Celestial Rune Sigils as all the BindRunes have been designed for ease of understanding and will take immediate effect upon use. Thus, they collectively function as The Metaphysician's Toolbox.

JOURNEY OF THE ENLIGHTENMENT SIGIL

Figure 3: The Enlightenment Sigil constructed from a BindRune containing the Ingwaz, Perth, Kaunan and Ihwaz Elder Futhark runes.

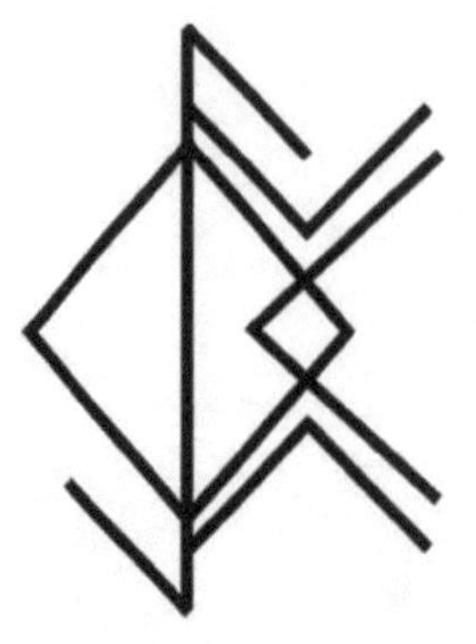

I seek harmony through the exploration of the unknown. Guide me to bring to light my shadow and it will enlighten my spiritual path.

The Enlightenment Sigil represents the universal idea behind the runes. It is drawn in a specific order (Figure 3), which follows; Ingwaz, Perth, Kaunan and Ihwaz. This binds the rune meanings of Peace, Mystery, Light and Magic.

The poem I have created for the BindRune "I seek harmony through the exploration of the unknown. Guide me to bring to light my shadow and it will enlighten my spiritual path." represents the order in which the seekers travels along his/her spiritual journey, where one has to plunge into the dark and unknown to emerge in the light during one's search of truth and harmony. This search is constant, a cycle that never ends and will continue throughout your life. This is an empowerment sigil, which you can call upon in your mind's eye at any time or can carve/draw on any object you wish to empower with your own personal energy or magick.

JOURNEY OF
THE WEAPON OF
LIGHT SIGIL

Figure 4: The Weapon of Light Sigil constructed from a Bin-dRune containing the Thurisaz, Sowilo and Kaunan Elder Futhark runes. It is connected to the Celestial and Earth currents.

I will seek and strike at

the enemies from my shadow.

My weapon will guide me and

bring to light my darkest shades.

The Weapon of Light is meant to be drawn in order (Figure 4), which follows: Thurisaz, Sowilo and Kaunan. This binds the rune meanings of Axe, Sun and Light. It is a personal weapon that can be maintained for long periods at a time without draining the seeker. All negative energy encountered is recycled into the Earth and returned to the Celestial current.

The poem I have created for the BindRune "I will seek and strike at the enemies from my shadow. My weapon will guide me and bring to light my darkest shades." invokes energy from the celestial current which is used to empower its blow. When the axe is used to strike against negative energy (during shadow work) it grounds the energy back into the Earth and recycles it through the Earth current returning it once again to the Celestial current (Figure 5).

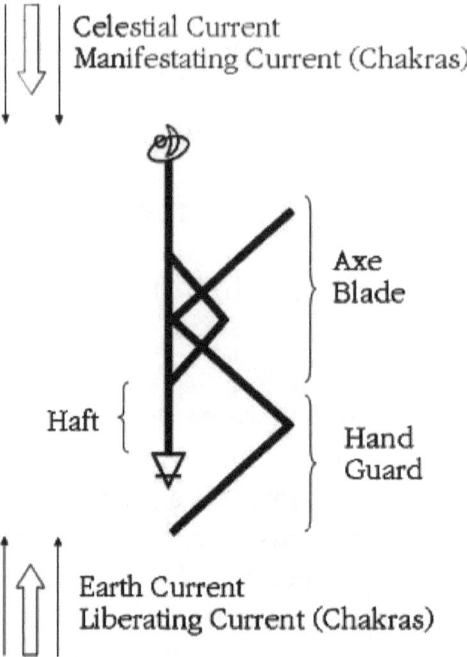

Figure 5: An illustration of the flow of energy when using the Weapon of Light Sigil. The Weapon is energized by the Celestial current and negative energy is grounded & recycled through the Earth current when striking.

Similar to the Shield of Light (in the next section), the Weapon of Light's design is influenced by the Germanic history of the Elder Futhark. Its imagery is meant to conjure that of an Iron Age Axe. The BindRune represents the main blade, hand guard and haft of the axe; with Thurisaz as the main weapon component (drawing upon its link to Mjölner, Thor's Hammer), Sowilo draws upon the energy of the sun and in conjunction with Kaunan forges the weapon with light.

The Astronomical and Alchemical Symbols draw upon the current of the universe via the Celestial Symbol (of my own design). The symbol's design was inspired by the Solar ☉ and Lunar ☽ symbols as well as the orbits of natural planetary satellites (i.e., moons).

It channels the incoming energy from the Celestial current (that represents both the stellar and planetary energies) and channels out energy through the Earth current to be grounded and re-cycled.

It is used in conjunction with the Shield of Light, since they constitute the Yin (Defensive, Shield, Left hand) and Yang (Assertive, Weapon, Right hand) of the Sigil. It can be invoked when conducting shadow work to protect the seeker and to light their spiritual journey through the depths to strike at the shade projections of the seeker's own mind and ego. The Shield of Light accompanies the Weapon and provides a torch to illuminate the enemy at which the Weapon must strike.

It is only meant to be used for personal protection (self-defense against negative energy or striking against your own shadow projections, whatever form they take) and not to harm another person for any reason.

Note: You can use the Solar ☉ or Lunar ☽ currents instead of the celestial current should it be more appropriate during the shadow work session or the spiritual ritual.

JOURNEY OF
THE SHIELD OF
LIGHT SIGIL

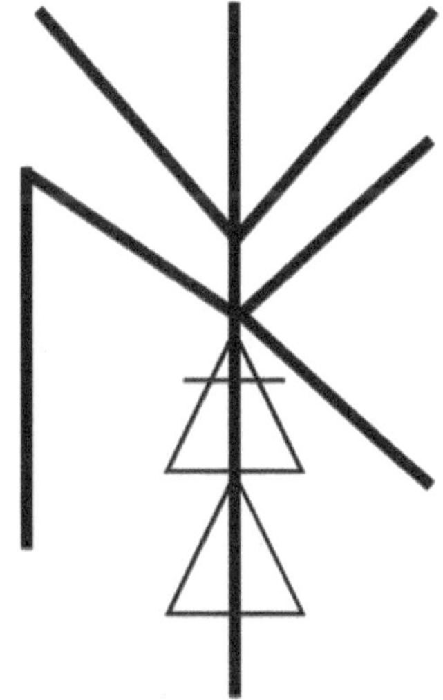

Figure 6: The Shield of Light Sigil constructed from a BindRune containing the Uruz, Algiz and Kaunan Elder Futhark runes. It is connected to the Fire and Air alchemical symbols.

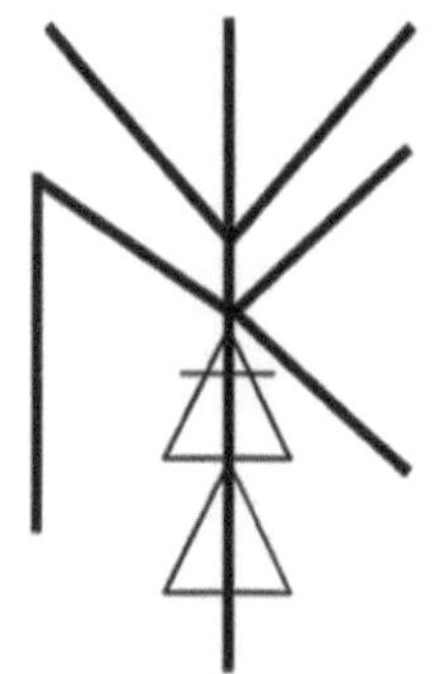

I will endure and repel

each strike from the shadow.

My shield will protect and

guide me through the darkness.

The Shield of Light is meant to be drawn in order (Figure 6), which follows: Uruz, Algiz and Kaunan. This binds the rune meanings of Force, Protect and Torch. It is a personal shield that can be maintained for long periods at a time without draining the seeker. All energy used is recycled into the Earth and returned to the Celestial current when used in conjunction with the Weapon of Light Sigil.

The poem I have created for the BindRune "I will endure and repel each strike from the shadow. My shield will protect and guide me through the darkness." links the Shield of Light to the Weapon of Light. The Shield of Light draws on the celestial current of light and energy as well as the liberating current from the earth. It creates a spherical shield around the seeker, which extends into the surrounding air and encases the seeker. Positive energy flows through the shield (visualization aids can include being surrounded by an O or B type main sequence star, such as Rigel or Bellatrix from the Orion constellation).

Similar to the Weapon of Light, the Shield of Light's design is influenced by the Germanic history of the Elder Futhark. Its imagery is meant to conjure that of an Iron Age Shield. The BindRune represents the main body of the shield (or base, suited to any shape the seeker desires); with Uruz for endurance and stamina, Algiz for steadfastness and Kaunan for light.

The Alchemical Symbols are its grip or enarmes; with Fire to channel energy from the Celestial and Earth currents (invoked in the Weapon of Light) and Air to permeate the space surrounding the seeker and holds the sphere in place. When struck with negative energy the Shield grounds or discharges the energy into the Earth, due to its access to the liberating current through the Weapon of Light (Figure 7).

Figure 7: An illustration of the flow of energy when using the Shield of Light Sigil. The Shield allows channelling of the Celestial & Earth currents when invoked by the Weapon of Light.

It is used in conjunction with the Weapon of Light, since they constitute the Yin (Defensive, Shield, Left hand) and Yang (Assertive, Weapon, Right hand) of the Sigil. It can be invoked when conducting shadow work to protect the seeker and light their spiritual journey through the depths as well as banishing negative energy (if you are in a confrontation with someone or need to interact with a difficult and/or draining person).

It is only meant to be used for personal protection (self-defense against negative energy or striking against your own shadow projections, whatever form they take) and not to harm another person for any reason.

JOURNEY OF THE SANCTUARY SIGIL

Figure 8: The Sanctuary Sigil constructed from a BindRune containing the Othila, Thurisaz, Tiwaz and Raido Elder Futhark runes.

Protect my family and friends,

and keep me from harm.

Protect us while at sea

and as we travel by land.

The Sanctuary Sigil is an universal area BindRune. It is meant to protect both yourself and your loved ones from harm. It provides protection as you travel (by sea, land or wheel) or when you stay in unfamiliar places. It is meant to be drawn in order (Figure 8), which follows: Othila, Thurisaz, Tiwaz and Raido. This binds the rune meanings of Family, Weapon, Protect and Travel.

The poem I have created for the BindRune "Protect my family and friends, and keep me from harm. Protect us while at sea and as we travel by land." invokes the rune's protective powers. You can use this as a travel amulet on your person or placed in your vehicle. It can also be used to protect an area, such as your room or house by hanging it on the doorknob or placing it at the entrance. It can also be used to imbue any object with protective qualities.

JOURNEY OF THE GUARDIAN SIGIL

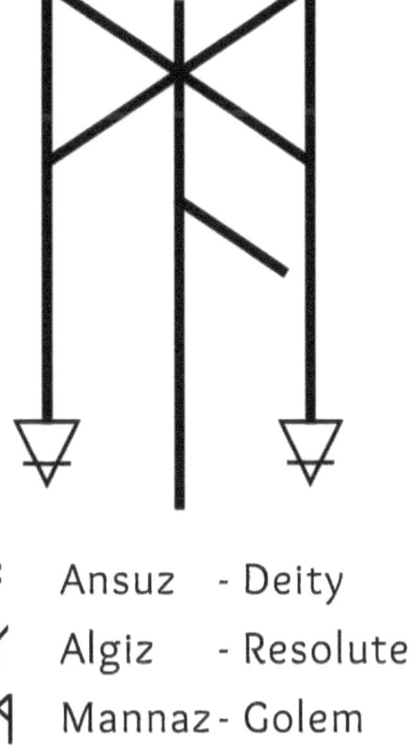

Figure 9: The Guardian Sigil constructed from a BindRune containing the Ansuz, Algiz and Mannaz Elder Futhark runes. It is connected to the Earth alchemical symbol.

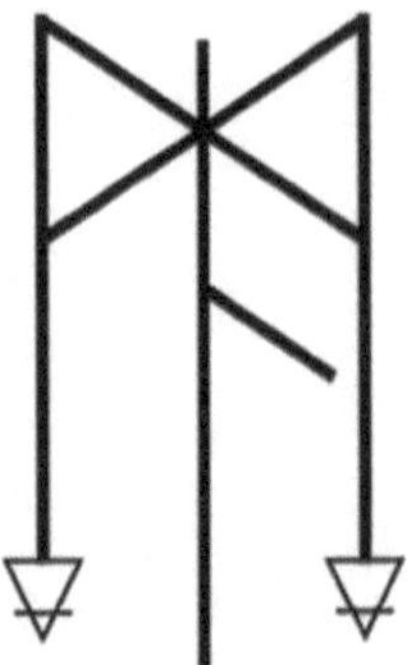

Sentinel of earth and

wisdom be present here.

Be my silent bastion

of spirit.

The Guardian Sigil is a personal spirit guardian. It is drawn in a specific order (Figure 9), which follows; Ansuz, Algiz and Mannaz. This binds the rune meanings of Deity, Resolute and Golem

The poem I have created for the BindRune "Sentinel of earth and wisdom be present here. Be my silent bastion of spirit." summons the Guardian of the Sigil. The guardian belongs to the realm of Odin, the Scandinavian god of war, wisdom, poetry and magick. It rises from the earth taking a humanoid form and hence one can visualize it as a crystal entity or golem of reflective light. It will silently guard your magickal and personal spiritual journeys.

JOURNEY OF THE NAVIGATION SIGIL

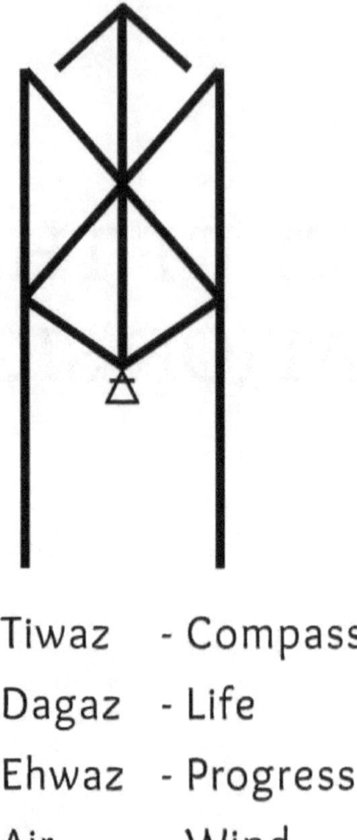

Figure 10: The Navigation Sigil constructed from a BindRune containing the Tiwaz, Dagaz and Ehwaz Elder Futhark runes. It is connected to the Air alchemical symbol.

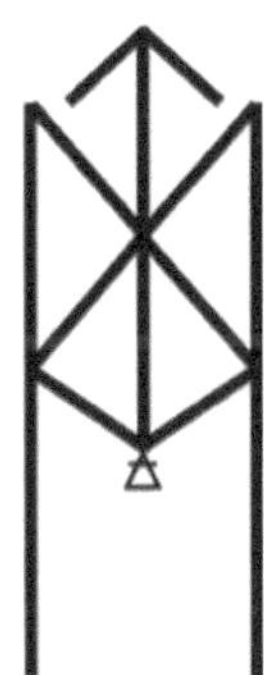

The wind is at my sails

and the sun is at my helm.

I will make my

own way forward.

The Navigation Sigil is an instrument of path finding. It is drawn in a specific order (Figure 10), which follows; Tiwaz, Dagaz and Ehwaz. This binds the rune meanings of Compass, Life and Progress.

The poem I have created for the BindRune "The wind is at my sails and the sun is at my helm. I will make my own way forward." sets the sails for your spiritual journey. It is similar to the navigational instruments used by sea-faring nations to travel around the world, such as the compass, the quadrant and the nocturnal. Many of these were also used in conjunction with the sun or stars; the Navigation Sigil points towards the next step in your journey using your spirit purpose as its North and your will for the air to your sails.

JOURNEY OF THE PATIENCE SIGIL

Figure 11: The Patience Sigil constructed from a BindRune containing the Isa, Naudiz, Berkanan and Jera Elder Futhark runes.

Let me cultivate the
virtues of nature.
Everything is accomplished
when each moment
is cherished.

The Patience Sigil acts as a gentle reminder that all things get done in their own time. It is drawn in a specific order (Figure 11), which follows; Isa, Naudiz, Berkanan and Jera. This binds the rune meanings of Pause, Review, Nurture and Reap.

The poem I have created for the BindRune "Let me cultivate the virtues of nature. Everything is accomplished when each moment is cherished." was inspired by the cultivation of virtues in the Eastern Philosophical traditions; where patience is one of the first and most challenging of skills to develop. The Patience Sigil will assist with this by reminding you of the rewards that you will reap when you allow goals to take the time necessary to develop and grow.

JOURNEY OF THE CLARITY SIGIL

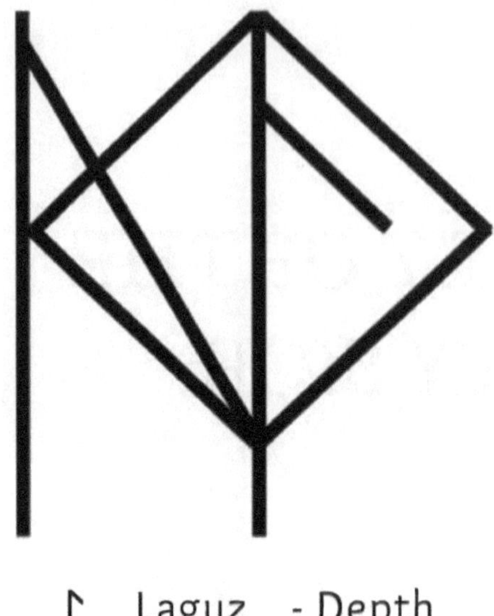

Figure 12: The Clarity Sigil constructed from a BindRune containing the Laguz, Hagalaz and Ingwaz Elder Futhark runes.

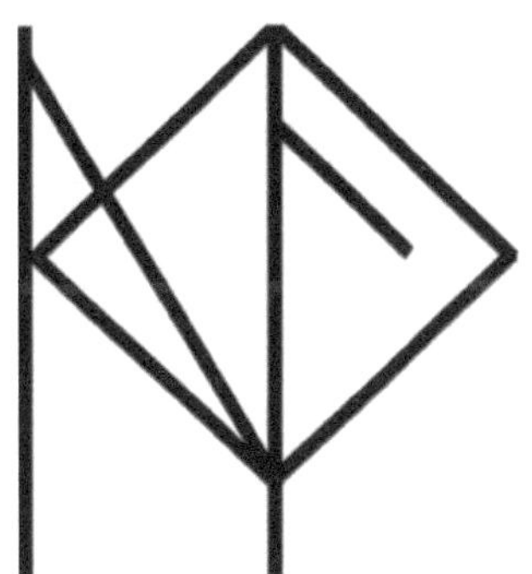

Allow me to be a visionary. Understand the depths of purpose and let them crystalize into my life.

The Clarity Sigil is tool of inspection. It is drawn in a specific order (Figure 12) which follows; Laguz, Hagalaz and Ingwaz. This binds the rune meanings of Depth, Crystal and Vision.

The poem I have created for the BindRune "Allow me to be a visionary. Understand the depths of purpose and let them crystalize into my life." illustrates that in life we require clarity for the short and long term. The Clarity Sigil can be used to evaluate both, much like a magnifying glass for closer inspection of immediate situations and it can be extended when one needs a telescope to view future plans.

JOURNEY OF THE GRACE SIGIL

Figure 13: The Grace Sigil constructed from a BindRune containing the Fehu, Gebo and Wunjo Elder Futhark runes.

May compassion be

my standard

and let me bestow good-will

to everyone I meet.

The Grace Sigil instills tolerance and understanding not only towards others but towards oneself. It is drawn in a specific order (Figure 13), which follows; Fehu, Gebo and Wunjo. This binds the rune meanings of Prosper, Generous and Gratitude.

The poem I have created for the BindRune "May compassion be my standard and let me bestow good-will to everyone I meet." recognizes that all people seek the same thing in life; happiness and fulfillment. When we place ourselves alongside them, envision their experiences we will learn to understand things from their point of view. This allows us to be less judgmental and harsh with those around us and then we learn to extend this onto ourselves.

JOURNEY OF THE
SPACE SIGIL

Figure 14: The Space Sigil constructed from a BindRune containing the Dagaz, Sowilo and Othila Elder Futhark runes.

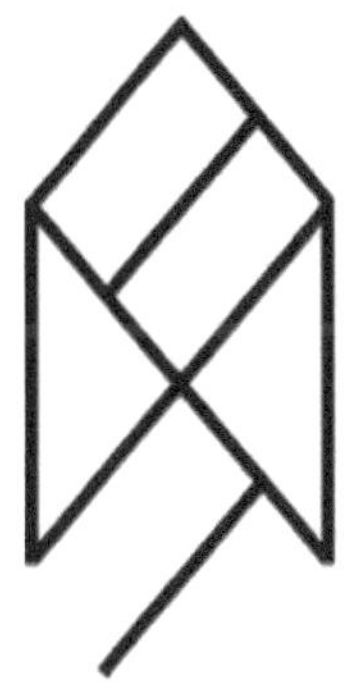

Through the voyage of

time and solitude

let the silence

bring me answers.

The Space Sigil represents meditation and mind space. It is drawn in a specific order (Figure 14), which follows; Dagaz, Sowilo and Othila. This binds the meaning of Sphere, Star and Holding which reminds us to not fear the silence.

The poem I have created for the BindRune "Through the voyage of time and solitude let the silence bring me answers." states that we all need to seek out solitude; this is where all the answers lie. It will not always be easy or what we would like to hear, but once we accept and integrate the truths we find during meditation; we will learn to become more at peace.

JOURNEY OF THE CHALLENGE SIGIL

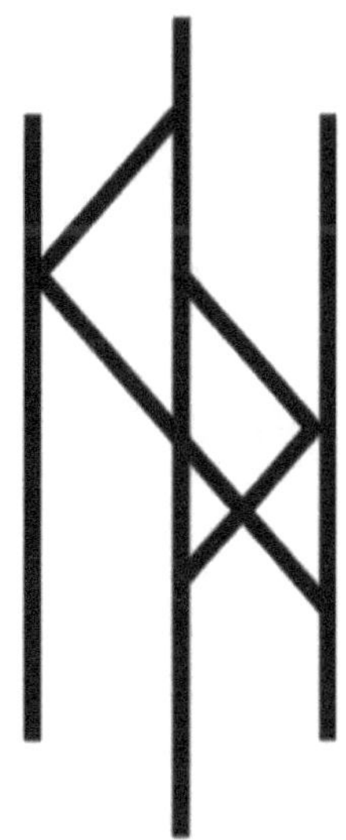

Figure 15: The Challenge Sigil constructed from a BindRune containing the Naudiz, Thurisaz, Jera and Hagalaz Elder Futhark runes.

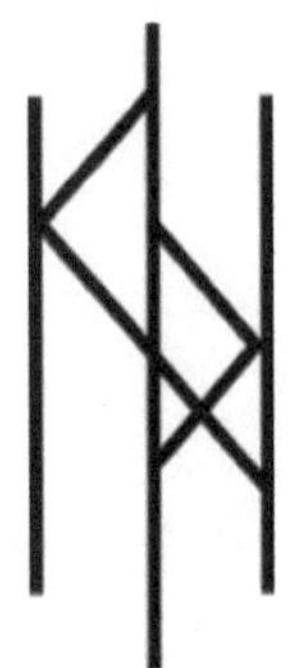

I will face my fears.

I will transform the

hurdles of life into

opportunities for growth.

The Challenge Sigil leads to opportunity and growth. It is drawn in a specific order (Figure 15), which follows; Naudiz, Thurisaz, Jera and Hagalaz. This binds the rune meanings of Hardship, Thorn, Yield and Change.

The poem I have created for the BindRune "I will face my fears. I will transform the hurdles of life into opportunities for growth." drives you forward to face opportunities. Challenging ourselves physically through exercise, emotionally through compassion, mentally through perspective changes and spiritually through meditation is uncomfortable and takes effort. The old adage "nothing worth doing is easy" applies to the Challenge Sigil. Challenge yourself and challenge others to invest more in themselves as well as investing in other people rather than in the material and the temporary.

JOURNEY OF THE HARMONY SIGIL

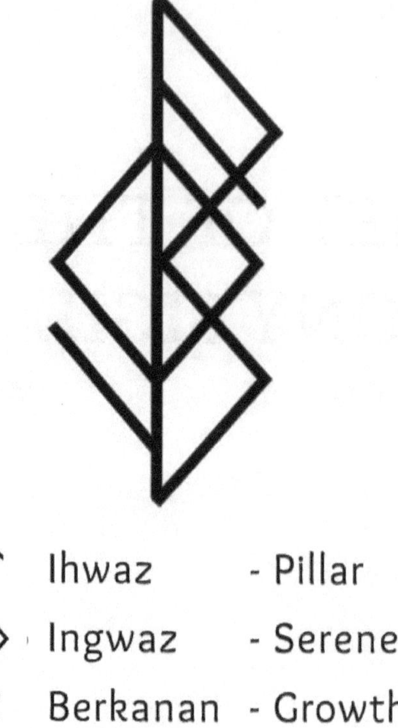

Figure 16: The Harmony Sigil constructed from a BindRune containing the Ihwaz, Ingwaz and Berkanan Elder Futhark runes.

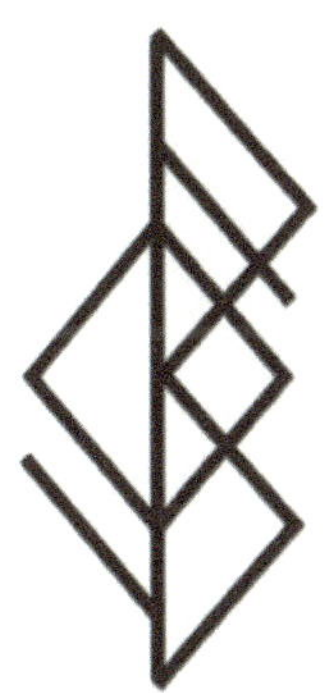

The only quest in life is for truth.

May it bring me

peace and happiness.

May it be the foundation of my life.

The Harmony Sigil is the true source of peace and happiness. It is drawn in a specific order (Figure 16), which follows; Ihwaz, Ingwaz and Berkanan. This binds the rune meanings of Pillar, Serene and Growth.

The poem I have created for the BindRune "The only quest in life is for truth. May it bring me peace and happiness. May it be the foundation of my life." indicates that we cannot function or live to our full potential when we are unbalanced. Seek to bring harmony to your life on all levels; physically by nurturing the body with healthy habits, emotionally by cultivating constructive habits, mentally through positive thinking and spiritually by facing your shadows and bringing them to light. The Harmony Sigil will assist you on this path.

JOURNEY OF THE DREAMS SIGIL

Figure 17: The Dreams Sigil constructed from a BindRune containing the Perth, Raido and Wunjo Elder Futhark runes.

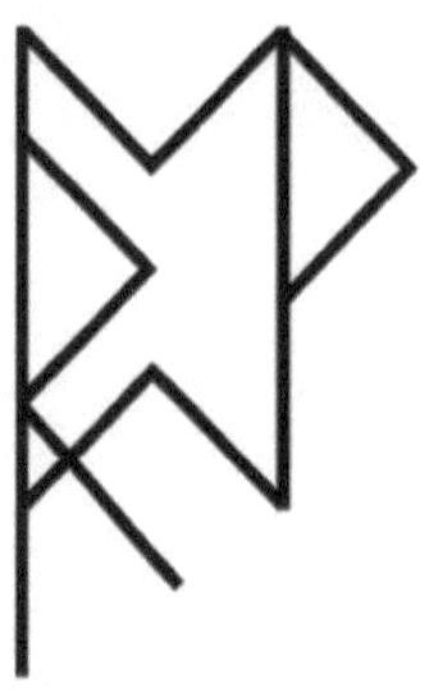

My deepest wishes take
flight at night.
Let me remember to
seek them out the in morning.

The Dreams Sigil reminds us of our desires in life and how far we have come. It is drawn in a specific order (Figure 17), which follows; Perth, Raido and Wunjo. This binds the rune meanings of Aether, Flight and Joy.

The poem I have created for the BindRune "My deepest wishes take flight at night. Let me remember to seek them out the in morning." speaks to the idea that the higher consciousness communicates through dreams, often using obscure symbols and parallels. Giving attention to these and figuring out their personal messages will guide you back to your authentic self. The Dream Sigil also shows us how far we have come and all the things we are grateful for.

JOURNEY OF THE INTUITION SIGIL

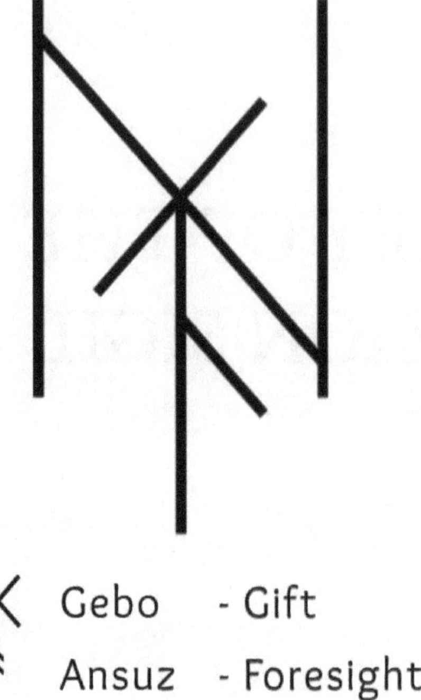

Figure 18: The Intuition Sigil constructed from a BindRune containing the Gebo, Ansuz and Hagalaz Elder Futhark runes.

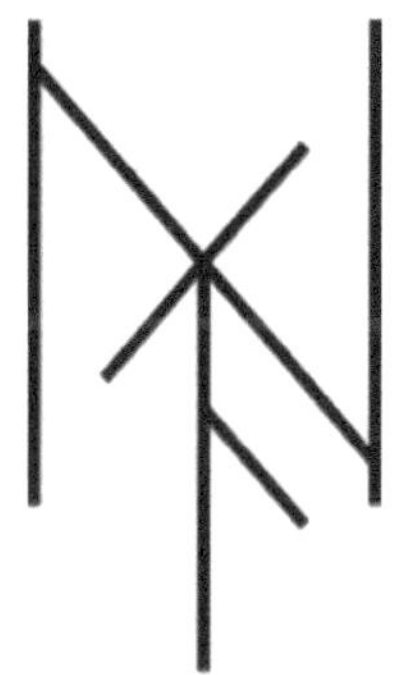

I should nourish the gift

as much as the rational mind.

Each is a part of me

and should be cherished.

The Intuition Sigil empowers your inner vision to cast light on the unseen. It is drawn in a specific order (Figure 18), which follows; Gebo, Ansuz and Hagalaz. This binds the rune meanings of Gift, Foresight and Morph.

The poem I have created for the BindRune "I should nourish the gift as much as the rational mind. Each is a part of me and should be cherished." reminds you to break away from structure and order, let the scientific and academic mind rest and try to see things with your creative side. "The intuitive mind is a sacred gift and the rational mind is a faithful servant. We have created a society that honors the servant and has forgotten the gift." - Albert Einstein.

JOURNEY OF THE FORTITUDE SIGIL

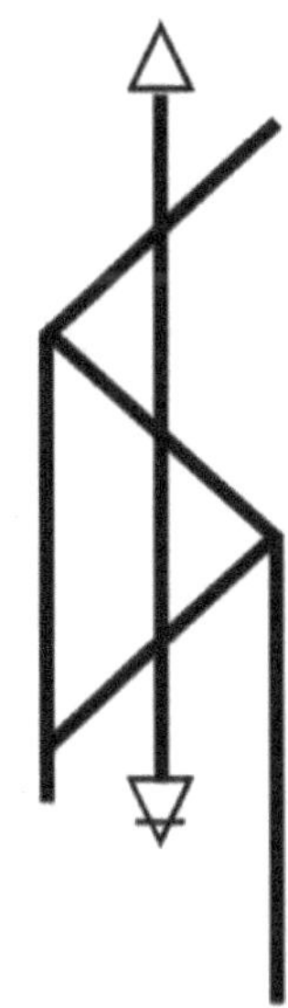

∫	Sowilo	- Strength
⋂	Uruz	- Endure
⨏	Naudiz	- Heed
△	Fire	- Heat
▽	Earth	- Rational

Figure 19: The Fortitude Sigil constructed from a BindRune containing the Sowilo, Uruz and Naudiz Elder Futhark runes. It is connected to the Fire and Earth alchemical symbols.

I seek strength in

times of need.

But temper my will

to fuel my understanding.

The Fortitude Sigil lends its strength in times of need. It is drawn in a specific order (Figure 19), which follows; Sowilo, Uruz and Naudiz. This binds the rune meanings of Strength, Endure and Heed.

The poem I have created for the BindRune "I seek strength in times of need. But temper my will to fuel my understanding." knows that we will face many challenges in life, all of which we can learn from and grow, but we require a bit of assistance during these times. Thus, the Fortitude Sigil will lend its ability to tap into your innate strength, powered by your deep well of soul and will allow you to rise after you have fallen. It is a balanced sigil and will allow assistance without becoming overbearing, without harming yourself or those around you.

JOURNEY OF THE INSPIRATION SIGIL

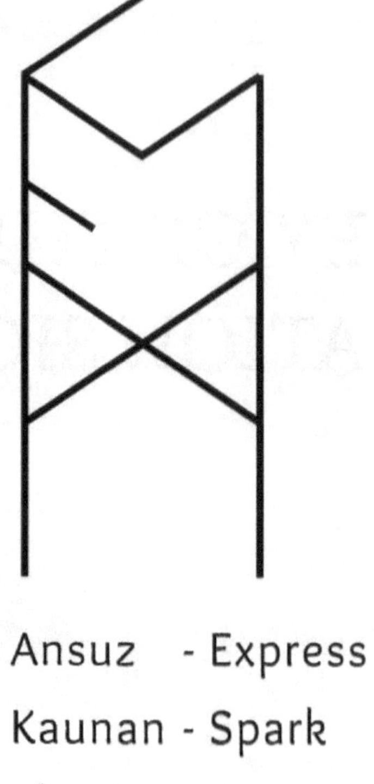

Figure 20: The Fortitude Sigil constructed from a BindRune containing the Ansuz, Kaunan, Ehwaz and Mannaz Elder Futhark runes.

The Inspiration Sigil pulls on your innate talents to create beauty and harmony. It is drawn in a specific order (Figure 20), which follows; Ansuz, Kaunan, Ehwaz and Mannaz. This binds the rune meanings of Express, Spark, Meet and Manifest.

The poem I have created for the BindRune "Let me tap into my mind to retrieve the knowledge I seek and set it free upon my waking hours." will act as your muse. Let your imagination take flight, break the rules, undo the shackles and experience true freedom.

JOURNEY OF THE
SPIRIT SIGIL

Figure 21: The Spirit Sigil constructed from a BindRune containing the Ehwaz, Perth and Othila Elder Futhark runes.

Allow me to unite my being at the seat of my spirit. Let its ancient wisdom guide my actions and thoughts.

The Spirit Sigil is the ultimate source of energy and grace. It is drawn in a specific order (Figure 21), which follows; Ehwaz, Perth and Othila. Cultivation of the soul is the only true focus in life. This binds the rune meanings of Union, Elements and Home.

The poem I have created for the BindRune "Allow me to unite my being at the seat of my spirit. Let its ancient wisdom guide my actions and thoughts." brings truth and reward through fulfillment and happiness. Our spirits should be nurtured as much as possible and should take part in everything we do every day.

JOURNEY OF THE INTROSPECTION SIGIL

Figure 22: The Introspection Sigil constructed from a BindRune containing the Isa, Perth and Mannaz Elder Futhark runes.

When I search within my

inner most being,

may I be guided towards

the path and towards myself.

The Introspection Sigil is the mirror we hold to our souls. It is drawn in a specific order (Figure 22), which follows; Isa, Perth, Mannaz. This binds the rune meanings of Reflect, Examine and Self.

The poem I have created for the BindRune "When I search within my inner most being, may I be guided towards the path and towards myself." reminds us that it is just as important to reflect upon your own actions and thoughts as much as it is to contemplate the world in which we live. Often solutions lie within.

JOURNEY OF THE HEALING SIGIL

Figure 23: The Healing Sigil constructed from a BindRune containing the Ihwaz, Uruz and Ingwaz Elder Futhark runes. It is connected to the Earth alchemical symbol.

Banish illness and dis-ease
from every facet of my being.
Guide me to the remedy
and teach me to heal.

The Healing Sigil reminds us to rest, mend and rejoice. It is drawn in a specific order (Figure 23), which follows; Ihwaz, Uruz and Ingwaz. This binds the rune meanings of Within, Power and Whole.

The poem I have created for the BindRune "Banish illness and dis-ease from every facet of my being. Guide me to the remedy and teach me to heal." states that all beings require rest to heal and mend the body, mind, emotions and the spirit. Far too often do we forget to take time to heal temporary cracks before they become permanent scars. The Healing Sigil reminds us to listen to our bodies and take the time to let ourselves heal.

JOURNEY OF THE REASON SIGIL

Figure 24: The Reason Sigil constructed from a BindRune containing the Perth, Tiwaz and Berkanan Elder Futhark runes.

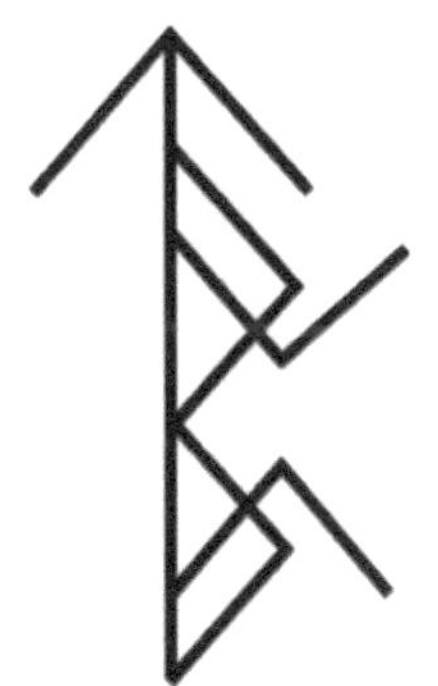

Let accuracy and sensibility be

guides to solutions.

Crafted by my own hand,

I resume control of my situation.

The Reason Sigil instills balanced perspectives as the foundation of our reality. It is drawn in a specific order (Figure 24), which follows; Perth, Tiwaz and Berkanan. This binds the rune meanings of Logic, Discipline and Develop.

The poem I have created for the BindRune "Let accuracy and sensibility be guides to solutions. Crafted by my own hand, I resume control of my situation." points out that often we create illusion in our lives by believing in unreasonable demands, of both ourselves and of others. The Reason Sigil reminds us to remain robust in our actions and thoughts, but not to become too rigid. Always keep an open mind to new experiences and knowledge.

JOURNEY OF THE TRUTH SIGIL

Figure 25: The Truth Sigil constructed from a BindRune containing the Othila, Ansuz and Algiz Elder Futhark runes.

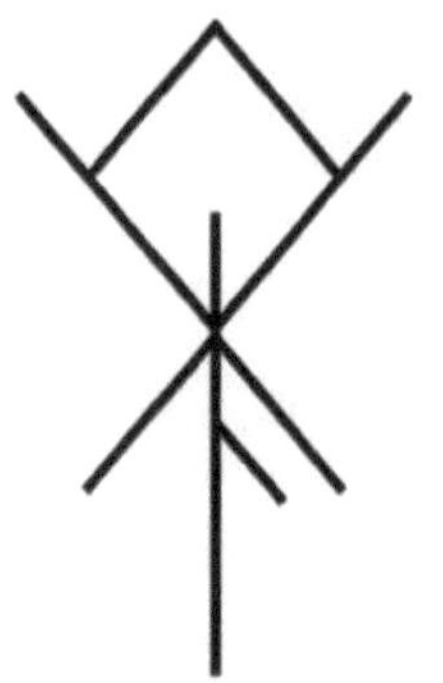

With clarity and devotion, let me distinguish the false from the real. Allow me the sight and recognition of genuine perspective.

The Truth Sigil allows us to find the truth and to trust what we have discovered. It is drawn in a specific order (Figure 25), which follows; Othila, Ansuz and Algiz. This binds the rune meanings of Comfort, Guidance and Keeper.

The poem I have created for the BindRune "With clarity and devotion, let me distinguish the false from the real. Allow me the sight and recognition of genuine perspective." illustrates a warrior of truth; it will show us whether something is real or false, whether it be a physical object, an uttered statement or even our own emotions and perspectives.

JOURNEY OF THE CLEANSING SIGIL

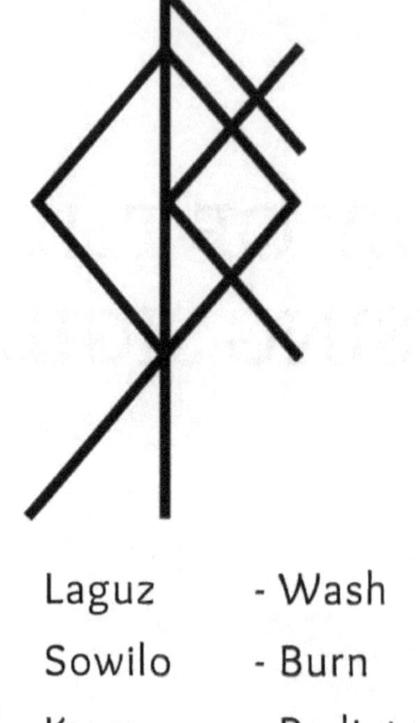

↑	Laguz	- Wash
ᛋ	Sowilo	- Burn
ᚲ	Kaunan	- Radiate
ᚦ	Thurisaz	- Excise

Figure 26: The Cleansing Sigil constructed from a BindRune containing Laguz, Sowilo, Kaunan and Thurisaz Elder Futhark runes.

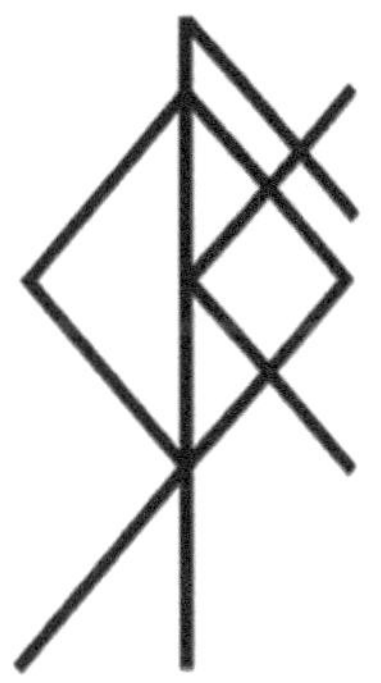

Dull my vision, blunt
my emotions. Tired my body, lost to
my soul. Purge my soot
and let me be renewed.

The Cleansing Sigil aids us to remove impurities and to cut away excess. It is drawn in a specific order (Figure 26), which follows; Laguz, Sowilo, Kaunan and Thurisaz. This binds the rune meanings of Wash, Burn, Radiate and Excise.

The poem I have created for the BindRune "Dull my vision, blunt my emotions. Tired my body, lost to my soul. Purge my soot and let me be renewed." knows that we often need to cleanse, recycle and repurpose - both our outer and inner worlds. Clean out the house and dust the cobwebs from your soul, remove what no longer serves and make space for the new perspectives that bring harmony.

JOURNEY OF THE PROJECT SIGIL

ᚠ	Fehu	- Work
ᚢ	Uruz	- Resilient
ᛟ	Dagaz	- Complete
ᛃ	Jera	- Reap

Figure 27: The Project Sigil constructed from a BindRune containing Fehu, Uruz, Dagaz and Jera Elder Futhark runes.

Give me strength of will

and dedication of effort.

Assist me to achieve all of that of

which I set out to accomplish.

The Project Sigil will help you to finalize unfinished projects, nurture ideas and to manifest concepts. It is drawn in a specific order (Figure 27), which follows; Fehu, Uruz, Dagaz and Jera. This binds the rune meanings of Work, Resilient, Complete and Reap.

The poem I have created for the BindRune "Give me strength of will and dedication of effort. Assist me to achieve all of that of which I set out to accomplish." is aware that we all have half-finished projects or some that have only just begun and even ones stuck at their conception. The Project Sigil will assist you in completing projects and seeing them through by tapping into your determination and instilling discipline.

JOURNEY OF THE FREEDOM SIGIL

Figure 28: The Freedom Sigil constructed from a BindRune containing Othila, Jera and Gebo Elder Futhark runes.

The Freedom Sigil reminds us of our most valuable endowment. It is drawn in a specific order (Figure 28), which follows; Othila, Jera and Gebo. This binds the rune meanings of Fate, Destiny and Will.

The poem I have created for the BindRune "Let my future, my past and my present harmonise and energize toward my common goal." asserts that we are not slaves of the past, nor pawns of the future; neither do we enforce our will with tyrannical might. We are empowered by our freedom of choice, which when harmoniously combined with our Fate, Will and Density has the power to lead us along our unique spiritual path of our own personal choosing.

OVERVIEW TABLES

Here I provide four quick reference tables with six sets of BindRunes, their poems and their construction. These are to assist you with crafting of the BindRunes during your magick rituals.

Table 1: A Quick Reference Table Of The First Set Of Six Bindrunes Of The Celestial Rune Sigils, Including The Enlightenment, Weapon Of Light, Shield Of Light, Sanctuary, Guardian And Navigation Sigils.

ENLIGHTENMENT		I seek harmony through the exploration of the unknown. Guide me to bring to light my shadow and it will enlighten my spiritual path.	Ingwaz – Peace Perth – Mystery Kaunan – Light Ihwaz – Magic
WEAPON OF LIGHT		I will seek and strike at the enemies from my shadow. My weapon will guide me and bring to light my darkest shades.	Thurisaz – Axe Sowilo – Sun Kaunan – Light Celestial Current Earth Current
SHIELD OF LIGHT		I will endure and repel each strike from the shadow. My shield will protect and guide me through the darkness.	Uruz – Force Algiz – Protect Kaunan – Torch Fire – Energy Air – Permeate
SANCTUARY		Protect my family and friends, and keep me from harm. Protect us while at sea and as we travel by land.	Othila – Family Thurisaz – Weapon Tiwaz – Shelter Raido – Travel
GUARDIAN		Sentinel of earth and wisdom be present here. Be my silent bastion of spirit.	Ansuz – Deity Algiz – Resolute Mannaz – Golem Earth – Rooted
NAVIGATION		The wind is at my sails and the sun is at my helm. I will make my own way forward.	Tiwaz – Compass Dagaz – Life Ehwaz – Progress Air – Wind

Table 2: A Quick Reference Table Of The Second Set Of Six Bindrunes Of The Celestial Rune Sigils, Including The Patience, Clarity, Grace, Space, Challenge And Harmony Sigils

PATIENCE		Let me cultivate the virtues of nature. Everything is accomplished when each moment is cherished.	Isa - Pause Naudiz - Review Berkanan - Nurture Jera - Reap
CLARITY		Allow me to be a visionary. Understand the depths of purpose and let them crystalize into my life.	Laguz - Depth Hagalaz - Crystal Ingwaz - Vision
GRACE		May compassion be my standard and let me bestow good-will to everyone I meet.	Fehu - Prosper Gebo - Generous Wunjo - Gratitude
SPACE		Through the voyage of time and solitude let the silence bring me answers.	Dagaz - Sphere Sowilo - Star Othila - Holding
CHALLENGE		I will face my fears. I will transform the hurdles of life into opportunities for growth.	Naudiz - Hardship Thurisaz - Thorn Jera - Yield Hagalaz - Change
HARMONY		The only quest in life is for truth. May it bring me peace and happiness. May it be the foundation of my life.	Ihwaz - Pillar Ingwaz - Serene Berkanan - Growth

Table 3: A Quick Reference Table Of The Third Set Of Six Bindrunes Of The Celestial Rune Sigils, Including The Dreams, Intuition, Fortitude, Inspiration, Spirit And Introspection Sigils

		Runes	
DREAMS	My deepest wishes take flight at night. Let me remember to seek them out the in morning.	Perth — Aether Raido — Flight Wunjo — Joy	
INTUITION	I should nourish the gift as much as the rational mind. Each is a part of me and should be cherished.	Gebo — Gift Ansuz — Foresight Hagalaz — Morph	
FORTITUDE	I seek strength in times of need. But temper my will to fuel my understanding.	Sowilo — Strength Uruz — Endure Naudiz — Heed Fire — Heat Earth — Rational	
INSPIRATION	Let me tap into my mind to retrieve the knowledge I seek and set it free upon my waking hours.	Ansuz — Express Kaunan — Spark Ehwaz — Meet Mannaz — Manifest	
SPIRIT	Allow me to unite my being at the seat of my spirit. Let its ancient wisdom guide my actions and thoughts.	Ehwaz — Union Perth — Elements Othila — Home	
INTROSPECTION	When I search within my inner most being, may I be guided towards the path and towards myself.	Isa — Reflect Perth — Examine Mannaz — Self	

Table 4: A Quick Reference Table Of The Fourth Set Of Six Bindrunes Of The Celestial Rune Sigils, Including The Healing, Reason, Truth, Cleansing, Project And Freedom Sigils

	Sigil	Invocation		Runes	
HEALING		Banish illness and dis-ease from every facet of my being. Guide me to the remedy and teach me to heal.	ᛁ	Ihwaz	- Within
			ᚢ	Uruz	- Power
			◇	Ingwaz	- Whole
			▽	Earth	- Grounded
REASON		Let accuracy and sensibility be guides to solutions. Crafted by my own hand, I resume control of my situation.	ᛈ	Perth	- Logic
			↑	Tiwaz	- Discipline
			ᛒ	Berkanan	- Develop
TRUTH		With clarity and devotion, let me distinguish the false from the real. Allow me the sight and recognition of genuine perspective.	ᛟ	Othila	- Comfort
			ᚨ	Ansuz	- Guidance
			ᛉ	Algiz	- Keeper
CLEANSING		Dull my vision, blunt my emotions. Tired my body, lost to my soul. Purge my soot and let me be renewed.	ᛚ	Laguz	- Wash
			ᛋ	Sowilo	- Burn
			ᚲ	Kaunan	- Radiate
			ᚦ	Thurisaz	- Excise
PROJECT		Give me strength of will and dedication of effort. Assist me to achieve all of that of which I set out to accomplish.	ᚠ	Fehu	- Work
			ᚢ	Uruz	- Resilient
			ᛞ	Dagaz	- Complete
			ᛃ	Jera	- Reap
FREEDOM		Let my future my past and my present harmonise and energize toward my common goal.	ᛟ	Othila	- Fate
			ᛃ	Jera	- Destiny
			✕	Gebo	- Will

LAST WORDS

After taking this journey with me and the Celestial Rune Sigils, I am sure that you have noticed a common theme throughout. That of Self-Empowerment.

This was the core focus surrounding the creation of the Celestial Rune Sigils as I believe that the greatest gift to ourselves (and subsequently to others) is that of self-reliance. When we actively seek out self-improvement and develop life skills, we become an unstoppable force and this empowers us to accomplish everything and endure anything with humility and grace. We also gladly share the knowledge we have acquired and help others along their journeys.

The Celestial Rune Sigils are tools, much like a healing crystal or a set of meditation beads. They are meant to assist you, not to make you dependent on them. Thus, the uses of these BindRunes may also change with time along your specific needs. They are not rigid and will grow with you as you further your journey to discover who you are and embrace your passions regardless of what the rest of the world thinks or prescribes.

I am grateful that you have chosen to set upon this spiritual journey with me! I hope that the Celestial Rune Sigils will act as your own personal Metaphysician's Toolbox as well and that they will provide invaluable assistance on your path as you glean insights from your own soul.

Blessings & Good Fortune

All Natural Spirit

* * *

BOOKS IN THIS SERIES

Runes

Runic Evolution & Linguistic History: The Origin Of The Germanic Runes & Universal Rune Sets

The Elder Futhark, Younger Futhark and Anglo-Saxon Futhorc are some of the most ancient writing scripts and collectively represent the runic alphabets of Germanic decent. In this book we explore the obscure and fascinating origins of these alphabets. We also observe how they evolved over time and their linguistic evolution due to influences from other languages. I also provide an overview for each set of runes (Elder Futhark, Younger Futhark and Anglo-Saxon Futhorc), which includes how I came to derive an historically accurate and universal rune set for each based on expert sources. The rune sets include the linguistically accurate letters, names and English transliterations. Even though I do not cover rune divination, I do discuss the context of rune magic from a historic perspective. Thus, this is not a divinatory book, but rather a historical reference to supplement both the metaphysical practitioners' and amateur runologists' knowledge and understanding of the runes.

Elder Futhark Arcanum: An Intuitive Interpretation Of Rune Meanings

Are you an open-minded spiritual practitioner? A seeker of truth and knowledge? Someone who is willing to discuss alternate perspectives? Then this book is for you.

Here within is my attempt at finding the truth behind the purpose and origin of the Elder Futhark as well as intuitively deciphering their somewhat obscure meanings.

At a glance this book provides:
* Discussion on how runes became a language used for divination
* Modern meaning interpretations for each rune
* Abstract geometric artwork for each rune
* Additional western alchemical and astronomical associations for each rune
* Several overview tables and references

In this context, this book does not discuss the traditional meanings or interpretations of the runes, but rather more modern outlooks and perspectives on each. Instead of adding more content to already confusing and conflicting traditional/conventional meanings – I have opted for the opposite, to simplify rather than complicate. I have tried to distill the core of each rune through my studies into their history, linguistics and metaphysics in order to make clear delineations between the runes. Thus, brief mentions are made to traditional meanings in favour of more discussion around the transference of the runes into our daily lives with reference to more familiar circumstances and challenges.

I am quite partial to the metaphysical symbolism of animals, plants and objects, thus this book includes plenty representations form the animal kingdom as well as everyday objects and some minor contributions from herbology. I have tried to keep to the mythology related to the Germanic tribes and to the everyday references of people living in Iron Age Europe. Therefore, some of my interpretations are similar to their traditional counterparts, but the majority of them have been cast anew.

I truly appreciate any review and feedback as I am constantly striving towards improving this runic body of work!

ABOUT THE AUTHOR

All Natural Spirit

I am a pathfinder, always setting onto unknown roads and discovering new perspectives. The knowledge I gain through my ad-
ventures allows me to create new systems
and innovate existing ones. I am a published
scientist in the life sciences with several
peer-reviewed academic journals. My scien- 
tific mind lends the discipline and structure to pursue my meta-
physical projects. I am also a certified Crystal Healing Practitioner
with the Sunshine Academy of Metaphysics. I created All Natural
Spirit as the public persona of my spiritual identity, because as a
scientist; I question the conservative and rigid thinking of modern day materialism and the close-minded dogma of academia.
All Natural Spirit (https://allnaturalspirit.com/) has manifested
as a website and blog where I regularly publish articles and even
a series of free oracle cards. I believe in open-source information
as well as disseminating complex scholarly or scientific studies to
the public by making it more relatable to a wider audience, hence
the creation of my books and art.

www.ingramcontent.com/pod-product-compliance
Lightning Source LLC
Chambersburg PA
CBHW031139250726
48655CB00002B/753